15-DAY DEVOTIONAL

# MOMENTS FOR *Moms*

## GIVE YOURSELF A MINUTE

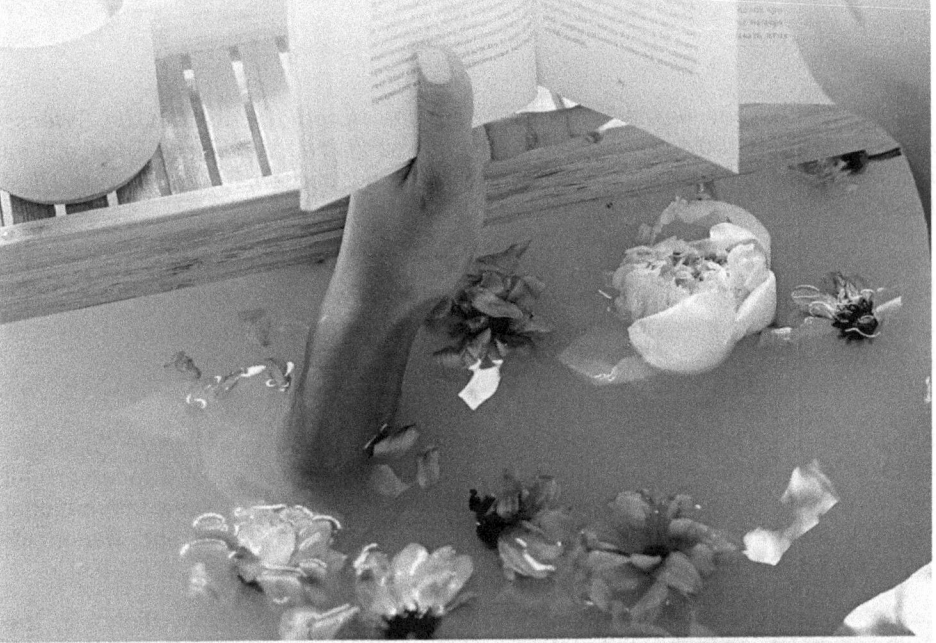

## JUANITA N. WOODSON

**WITH CO-AUTHOR APPEARANCES BY**
AUJAHNAE COADY, CATRINA JACKSON, CYTEESE ALEXANDER,
CHERYL BOWMAN, EBONY S. BAILEY, RONJEANNA HARRIS,
NIKKI LAWRENCE, SHANICE SPENCE, LISA FREEMAN,
SHATERA MARTZ, MARQUESE HANNAH,
JACCARRI WOODSON, TONISHA MORTON

Copyright © 2022 by Juanita N. Woodson, AuJahna'e Coady, Catrina Jackson, Cyteese Alexander, Cheryl Bowman, Ebony Bailey, Ronjeanna Harris, Shanice Spence, Lisa Freeman, Shatera Martz, Marquese Hannah, JAcarri Woodson, Tonisha Morton, Nikki Lawrence

No parts of this book may be reproduced without written approval from complier, Juanita Woodson, or any co-author, except for excerpts to be used for reviews or press releases.

Scriptures taken from the Holy Bible, New International Version®, NIV®. Copyright © 1973, 1978, 1984, 2011 by Biblica, Inc.™ Used by permission of Zondervan. All rights reserved worldwide. www.zondervan.com The "NIV" and "New International Version" are trademarks registered in the United States Patent and Trademark Office by Biblica, Inc.™

Scripture quotations from The Authorized (King James) Version. Rights in the Authorized Version in the United Kingdom are vested in the Crown. Reproduced by permission of the Crown's patentee, Cambridge University Press

ISBN (paperback) - 979-8-9861363-8-7

**Published in the United States by Grace 4 Purpose, Publishing Co. LLC**
www.grace4purposeco.com
Interior Format: Purposely Booked Publishing
Book cover design by Untouchable Designz and Consulting.

*Printed and bound in the United States of America*

# Table of Contents

Dedication | 5

Day One- Ebony S. Bailey | 9

Day Two- Catrina Jackson | 15

Day Three- Marquese Hannah | 21

Day Four- AuJahna'e Coady | 27

Day Five- Nikki Lawrence | 33

Day Six- Shatera Martz | 39

Day Seven- Lisa Freeman | 45

Day Eight- Cheryl Bowman | 55

Day Nine- Shanice Spence | 59

Day Ten- Tonisha Morton | 65

Day Eleven- Jaccarri Woodson | 71

Day Twelve- Cyteese Alexander | 75

Day Thirteen- RonJeanna Harris | 81

Day Fourteen- Juanita N. Woodson | 87

Day Fifteen- Give Yourself a Minute Mama | 93

# Dedication

This book is dedicated to every mom, grandmother, and mother figure who deserves to give themselves a minute. We often feel that we aren't allowed to take a break, and we are here to remind you that you deserve to give yourself a minute, mama.

# Are you ready to give yourself the *Moment* you deserve?

---

## Let's get started!

Moments for Moms
*Ebony S. Bailey*

# Day One

Hey Mama! My name is *Ebony S. Bailey*. I am a wife, mom, author strategist, creative, and purpose enthusiast who challenges women wake up and walk in their God-given purpose, on purpose. I do this through my published books, journals, She Woke Up web series, and more. I remind women that they can physically have everything they see in their dreams. Each dream is achievable by divine connection to God and man, with intention, goal setting, discipline, and belief in yourself. My goal is to challenge you to walk towards your purpose with fervency, commitment, and passion because destiny is waiting for YOU!

One thing that has presented itself as a challenge since I became a mother at the age of 20 is staying present. The older I become, the more I have to work on not allowing the duty of being a mom (along with the many other hats I wear) to overshadow the privilege it is. It's extremely easy to get lost in building a life and legacy for my kids that they and God can be proud of. Unfortunately, my goal-oriented nature sometimes causes me to have tunnel vision, consequently causing me to miss out on enjoying and creating many unique and memorable moments with them.

I have five children aged 7 – 18 years old. And trust me, my household is far from quiet. Even among the busyness, I still have to fight against tuning everyone out and retreating into a place of solitude. I'd be lying if I didn't say I am consistently working at this! Listen, I am a natural introvert who enjoys quiet and being alone most of the time. However, I know that it is vital to slow down and be involved in the things that bring me joy and the things that bring them happiness. Each child is different and requires a different combination to unlock the treasures inside of them. The only way to identify as a parent is to pay close attention to them and spend time understanding their personality and individuality outside of being "your child." (We can forget that there is a difference.)

*The first thing* I had to do was slow down and listen to my children. I learned I wasn't loving and showing up for two of my daughters the way they needed. (That hurt!) One showed me how she internalized her emotions, which caused her to be sad and emotional for a season. The other didn't want to share her thoughts because she didn't think it would change anything. Finally, I had to say, Ebony, your daughters speak without using words, and it is up to you to interpret what they are trying to communicate.

*The second thing* I had to do was acknowledge I wasn't loving them the way they needed to be loved and nurtured; this was tough! As a mom, allowing this reality to infiltrate your emotions can make you feel like you failed. However, the truth is, it's not. The problem arises when you ignore their feelings, creating more hurt, which makes an even more significant issue.

*The third thing* was reminding myself to be intentional about learning the individual needs of each of my children so I could effectively show up for them. I reflected on when my husband and I were on different pages, and we listened to *"The Five Love Languages"* by Gary Chapman and got things back on track. I found that the same author wrote a love language book for children, and I immediately downloaded it. It opened my eyes even more to how to serve and parent my children!

opened my eyes even more to how to serve and parent my children! If I wanted to show up and be active and present in their daily lives, I had to be open to new ways of loving them. I had to adjust my priorities and not just focus on setting them up for the future but on learning how to enjoy life with them in a way that matter in their eyes. I had to open up dialogue, stop making assumptions, refrain from interrupting them when they spoke, and not respond with judgment or a harsh tone. I had to tell them how important and valuable perspective is while proving it with my actions. So now that I have stepped back and evaluated my interactions, I am working on perfecting my tone and setting aside quality time with them together and individually.

It is my goal (and should be the goal of every parent) to teach their children who they are so the world does force their opinions and labels on them. I have realigned my life to be present, aware, and alert of my children's emotional, physical and spiritual needs.

**Here are a few things that helped me work on becoming more in tune with myself and my children:**

**1. Have a morning routine.** This saved my life! Making sure I start my day with God, whether in prayer, reading, devotional time, meditation, or listening to worship music, helps me get centered and geared up for my day. During this time, I am building my spirit while reminding myself of the things God has spoken to me. Consequently, reassuring myself that it shall come to pass because God is not a man that He should lie. I take this time to listen for direction from God for my day, and after I walk out of that time, I feel at peace because I know I have given Him the better part of my day!

**2. Watch your mouth!** I am a firm believer that your words shape your world. We are natural creators; the Word of God tells us in Proverbs 18:21 that life and death are in the power of the tongue. We can

can literally use our words to build up or tear down. Even on challenging days, I am learning it is essential to watch what you say because each word out of your mouth has an assignment. I try my very best to speak affirmations over myself AND my family. I do my best to cover them in prayer daily. One of the things I speak over them is: "I clothe my children in the armor of God until they know how to dress themselves in the spirit."

3. **It is okay to have an off day.** I think we as moms put too much pressure on ourselves to be perfect and superhuman. We do not allow ourselves the time or space, to be honest with the emotions we are experiencing. I know we have all heard, "It is okay not to be okay," and my friend, that is nothing short of the truth. Give yourself the space, to be honest with how you feel. I am not telling you to wallow there but experience the emotion and pick yourself back up. Our families will love us through the different stages and phases of life. Remember, you deserve every moment you need to be healed, healthy, and whole!

To learn more about me, *Ebony S. Bailey,* my products, services, and resources, visit **ebonysbailey.com** or connect with me on social media: **Instagram and Facebook** @ ebsbailey.

• • • • • • • • • • • • • • • • • • • • • • •

*How did this relate to you? Jot it down below.*

**Moments for Moms**
*Catrina Jackson*

# Day Two

### *Breathe, Heal, Overcome!*

*"⁸ "-Then your light shall break forth like the morning, your healing shall spring forth speedily, and your righteousness shall go before you; The glory of the LORD shall be your rear guard." (Isaiah 58; 1-14).*

Hello Beautiful Mama! If you haven't already today, take a deep breath in... now exhale slowly. It helps right? My name is Catrina; wife for ten years, mother of three wonderful children, budding author, editor and copywriter, daughter, sister, friend, mentor, homeschooler... and without even knowing you personally, I know you are wearing many of those hats and then some! It's what we Mama's do and why rallying around each other, if for no other reason than just to remind you to breathe. If you're like me and get intermittently overwhelmed, another Mama friend told me to put my oxygen mask on first. On a plane during the safety speech, they always remind you in case of losing cabin pressure, to put your mask on first because if you pass out trying to help someone else... we know the outcome. For today's devotional, let's talk about inner healing.

*Inner healing is just one of the many ways God has graced us to show His love.* None of us Mama's would leave a wound unattended on our babies. Depending on the type of wound will determine the recommended treatment and if we admit it, there are times we do not let the Lord, or anyone else, get close to the wound. Sometimes it is because we are afraid of further injury. Other times, we think we have healed just fine, only for a triggering event to remind us that we are still vulnerable, and that wound is still festering. That was me for a while. Suffering childhood sexual abuse led to promiscuity in my teens and twenties and now at forty-two, the memories have faded, but the effects are still there. Control issues, claustrophobia, random crying, withdrawal, and depression. You may know what that feels like or know someone who is going through it.

**Overcomer STEP 1:** "By the blood of the lamb and the words of our testimonies." (Rev. 12:11) We receive the healing made available to us by the blood of Jesus and we share our stories to spread hope!

**Overcomer STEP 2:** "But as for me and my house, we will serve the Lord." (Josh. 24:14-15) Sometimes our inner healing and deliverance is simply deciding that we chose the Lord over our emotions. We sang "I have *decided* to follow Jesus" as children and now decide to give Him whatever you are feeling or need from Him taking it one day at a time.

**Overcomer STEP 3:** "Submit to God, resist the devil and he will flee." (James 4:7) In that order! If you need the torment to stop and you have tried to resist the devil and the temptation to sin, you are fighting a losing battle without God. "Seek Him first and His righteousness" (Matt. 6:33; not your "but I'm a good person" point of view of righteousness), put on the full armor of God (Eph. 6) and then you will be equipped to withstand all the fiery darts of your past trauma or current wilderness.

Take that same energy you use to go off in defense of your family for yourself when confronting the enemy of your soul. Confront the spiritual enemy, forgive the person(s) who hurt you, and repent of anything hindering the will of God in your life. Then walk fully in the purpose God has given you... and if you don't know what that is, you know it isn't for defeat! You can do hard things! *Encourage yourself in the Lord. Write to tell me all about it at <u>hello@rolecall.faith</u>!*

Moments For Moms - *Catrina Jackson*

Give yourself a *Moment!*

*How did this relate to you? Jot it down below.*

Moments for Moms
*Marquese Hanna*

# Day Three

    Hello, Mommie's! My name is Marquese Hannah. I was born in New Jersey, but then our family moved to Williamsburg, Virginia where we currently reside. I have a medical background and I worked in the healthcare field for about five years before becoming a stay-at-home mom, which I will tell you all about.

    As a first-time mom, I had huge struggles straight out of the gate into motherhood. My daughter was born two months early due to me having severe preeclampsia. I was sent to the hospital because my obstetrics doctor said I would be given a steroid to keep my daughter growing until her due date. When I arrived, they were just doing a routine check on the baby when they couldn't find a heartbeat. Turns out, my daughter's heart rate slowed down to the same beat as my heart. The doctor said that instead of being given a steroid, they would be performing an emergency c-section under anesthesia, talk about scared! On top of that, the surgery took place so fast that neither my mother nor my daughters' father was able to make it to the hospital for her birth. I was all alone, or so I thought. There was a nurse there who asked the doctor to be present with me just to hold my hand through it all, God truly sent an angel. The battle was far from over because my daughter would be in Nicu for twenty-eight days. Throughout that time, I visited her everyday. Every time the nurses would say something negative about the progression of my daughter, God showed up and showed out! A child being born as early as she was, and the complications surrounding it, it is unheard of that a child would leave a NICU in less than thirty days; only God!

Another huge struggle that I endured was the dreadful postpartum depression. The crazy part about that struggle was, I had no idea I was even going through it until a few months after having my daughter home. I was emotional, and severely depressed, and after all that God had done, I found myself asking "Why me?" Well as you can see, if you're reading this, that is why I went through what I went through, it was for you and any other mother who has experienced what I have experienced. I got through the struggle of a premature daughter and postpartum depression by not only remembering the prayers and promises of God, but the village I call my family. I never was a woman to lean on anyone else or depend on people because I was so independent, but honey, I had no choice but to lean on family during that time. I also had friends who I call sisters now who joined my village during that time because I was in a whole new arena called motherhood, and they already were mothers, so they knew how to lift me up. Most people think postpartum gives you separation from your child, and that can be the case for some, but not for me. I was close with my daughter during all of it, it was the separation within myself that I was battling. I received God-sent wisdom and advice from mothers in all stages of life, they helped me find my way back to myself.

**If I can leave you with three pieces of advice it would be this:**

*1. Take time to rest and renew yourself.* Rejuvenation goes a long way when you take care of yourself. If you are fortunate to have a reliable, safe person in your life to give you a break with your little one, take it, and rest.

*2. It is ok to feel how you feel.* One thing I did not do was let anyone make me feel like what I felt wasn't valid. No matter how I felt, it was real, and it was ok to feel that way. God was always there to show himself through the doubts, anger, and sadness, just through it all. It helped build my faith in Him even more because of it all.

**3. Lean on your spouse. If he is not present, lean on your family if you can.** They are not there to harm you but to help you, and you have to let them. Help does not mean you are weak or unable, it just means that you are strong enough to place yourself in someone else's hands to be cared for. No matter what you do, just let someone be there for you.

I hope that you have found something I've said to be helpful to you on your beautiful journey of motherhood. Motherhood is a process, and no one's process looks the same so make sure you don't put yourself in a slump trying to compare. We are all on different journeys, but we can all learn from and help each other along the way. From my heart to yours, much love, and God bless you.

IG: reign_duchess_reign

Give yourself a
*Moment!*

*How did this relate to you? Jot it down below.*

Moments for Moms
*AuJahna'e Coady*

# Day Four

My name is AuJahna'e Coady also known as 'Thee Soul Writer.' I am a published Author, Motivational Speaker, and Healing Empowerment Coach. I own the podcast show Soul Writing Speaks on all platforms. I also mentor individuals to assist with self-development, healing trauma, and adversity. I am a mental health advocate and finally a loving mother.

We as mothers face adversity, struggles, and storms daily so there are never too many things we can hear to make ourselves feel better. To any mother that reads this: It's kind of hard to narrow it down to one struggle. The thing is, everyone expects mothers to be a superwoman, but it's really a pain behind being everything. So, I'll take this time to be completely transparent. You know the saying "a mother's job is never done," I know we all find ourselves saying that quite too often. One struggle I have being a mother is holding it all together when I'm on the verge of breaking a million times. Trying to be strong in front of your child gets overwhelming when you are who they look up to. You don't want them to see you in that form, so you shove it down. Here's how I've been able to hold it all together and still be the best mother I can be to my son at the same time:

There's no manual or 'how to' guide on being a mother but, it's one of those titles that isn't easy and comes with many risks and lessons. The day you become a mother, your whole life changes. You are no longer living for just you. It seems like soon as I became a mother, my adversity began coming left and right. I was facing storm after storm. The thing is my son was young at the time, so he had no understanding of what I was going through. The only pain he could sense was my emotions during the nights I spent holding him and crying. The warmth of his cuddles just felt so relieving at the time. As he got older though, my son could sense when I was off and upset. So, I had to find alternatives to how I would handle adversity and my emotions. I could no longer do the unhealthy things I was doing because he would begin to pick up on those traits. I didn't want my child to have to deal with generational trauma because I couldn't properly handle my adversity, so I decided to take action. It was not an easy process but, if you are a mother facing adversity first things first, IT IS OKAY! We have the right to go through things and we have the right to feel every emotion. We have that right to break every now and then, but we must remember to pick ourselves back up. Even if that includes reaching out for help.

    I know we love to be independent, strong, resilient, and many other things, but a broken mother cannot properly care for her child. This causes childhood trauma resulting in your child needing to be healed later down the line. Ignoring adversity like it isn't there or shoving it down causes a volcano just waiting to erupt. I know we have all had instances where we bottle so much in and then it explodes at the wrong moment because it could no longer be held. You don't have to always be strong because this eventually causes emotional damage to yourself, and your kids may become your target of release. You don't have to always have it together or know the right answers but that is what your village is for. As mothers, we need a village, a support system to uplift us when we can't do it ourselves. We need to have the courage to speak up when the opportunity presents itself. We need to also welcome another mother with open arms instead of judging the situation because the tables turn. Any mom can endure adversity but not every mom has the courage to ask for help and arise above the situation. Let's shift the narrative and chain together because together we are more powerful. Things that can help when life seems so overwhelming for me included long soaking baths, exercise, yoga, meditation, praying, change of scenery, and focusing on what am I supposed to learn from the situation. Just take a moment to evaluate what is at hand and how you will handle it. I had to accept the fact that I would never be the perfect mother to my son so I decided to be the best that I can be in my most healed form. If that meant asking for help, I did it. If it meant taking a mental break and getting myself together alone, I asked my village to watch him. If it meant taking time to understand why he would act the way he did or why he was crying I would allow him to communicate his emotions so that I could understand better. I allowed him the same communication because it made our relationship healthier and easier to manage. Parents can make the relationship just as difficult when they try and overrule and do not allow the child to express themselves. It gets easier the more it is practiced and has become an effective way for me and my son. So to the mother that reads this: remember to take it day by day and to also take care of yourself so that you can properly care for your children.

**To any mothers out there I'll say these three things:**

1. ***It is okay not to know all the right answers.*** It is okay to make mistakes, no one is perfect. It is okay to fall but it is not okay to stay down.
2. ***Live your life how you want*** because you still have a life to live after you become a mother, just be cautious of what you expose your little ones to.

3. ***Cherish every little moment you have with your kids*** because the one thing that you can't get back, is time, so enjoy it.

• • • • • • • • • • • • • • • • • • • • • • • • • • • • • •

IG: @thesoulwriterslegacy

Facebook: AuJahnae Coady

www.soulwritingllc.org

Podcast: Soul Writing

*How did this relate to you? Jot it down below.*

Moments for Moms
*Nikki Lawrence*

# Day Five

Hi Mama's, my name is Nikki Lawrence, and I am a Doctoral student, mother of two daughters, and an HR Analyst. I was born and raised in Williamsburg, VA and I have served on several committees to inspire others. I am also the co-owner of the LLC Pearls with a PROMISE. Pearls with a PROMISE is a mentoring group for young girls ages 9-20. While in pursuit of my Doctoral Degree, I have counseled many families, children, and victims of domestic violence. I am an almost 40-year-old mom, and I am looking forward to a lasting and committed career as a community activist.

One struggle I have had as a mother is this thing called 'Saving Face.' I have always been the one to raise my girls a certain way. Prayer every night, dinner by 5 pm, homework at 7 pm then shower and bed by 9 pm. On Sundays, we would fast until church was over. I made my girls respectful, I taught them how to show reverence to God, treat everyone kindly and love each other no matter what. Unfortunately, I didn't factor in the curve balls that life consistently throws. Who would have known that one of my daughters would be raped and the other would be angry all the time because she missed her sister? NO ONE. We never prepared for tragedies or heartbreak. I just made sure that we kept up appearances. You would never see us unkept, I would never discipline them outside of the home. We held up a standard of holiness and completeness. On the inside, I struggled to deal with my daughter's constant ups and downs from her assault, and my youngest daughter's temper tantrums. I was scared for the world to see us until one day I didn't care anymore because no one was getting healed.

The biggest step was letting my EGO go. I had to come to the realization that it's not always going to be cute, but it will be true. I made more time for the ugly moments instead of covering them up. I had tough conversations with my daughters that I knew would hurt. As mothers, we think we are doing things great, and to our children, we are failing. We sometimes are not as gentle as we should be. Not as kind or patient and we forget that the world has changed. I also started dating my daughters, together and individually. I started to focus on our goals as a whole and the biggest goal was their happiness.

*1) It doesn't always have to look pretty because God blesses what we think is a mess.*

*2) It's okay not to always be okay.* Being a mother is a new job every day and as soon as we think we have it down, life comes and smacks us with another challenge.

*3) Know that after you have raised your children, all that they do is not your fault.* Be at peace knowing that the prayers you prayed while your child was in the womb will manifest and God will keep His promise.

• • • • • • • • • • • • • • • • • • • • • • • • • • • • • • • •

Email: drlawc21@gmail.com

IG @ speaksvolumescounselingfirm

# Give yourself a
*Moment!*

*How did this relate to you? Jot it down below.*

Moments for Moms
*Shatera Martz*

# Day Six

Hi Ladies! My name is Shatera Martz, and I was born and raised in Dover, DE, and I now reside in Magnolia, DE with my husband Chris, and our five children. I am an author, relationship coach, and entrepreneur. I am a woman who is not afraid to use my faith to allow God to guide the direction of my life. By using my faith and own firsthand experiences, I encourage women, mothers, and wives who struggle with family dynamics.

One struggle I have had as a mother was keeping it fair as possible by dividing my time between five children. As a wife we learn how to be available for our husbands and going into motherhood we learn to divide that time with more than one person. There are incredible women who start off dividing time with their children before settling into a relationship. Whatever the case, keeping up with more than one child is a job, just for our children to still feel as though they are not important enough for our time at the end of the day. The truth is we are not always going to divide our time evenly with the people that we love for many reasons, however, we can take advantage of the moments and opportunities that present themselves to us daily.

When I was growing up, my mother had five children and I watched her struggle trying to give us the best of herself, even when she did not feel it. I witnessed how my mother divided her time with her school children, my dad, siblings, family, and friends and still have time to answer any questions I had. This is my story, but I know others may not have been fortunate as I, or some had the attention of their parents. As children, we do not always see how much of a task it is for a mother to divide her attention between her family and the world. When I became a parent, it was hard enough to share my life with my first-born child and when I met my husband and our three bonus children, I failed miserably in trying to connect with everyone equally. Besides all my efforts, it was also draining trying to split my time evenly as possible.

What is working for myself, and our family is taking advantage of every moment possible and every opportunity that presents itself to make the most of whatever situation and the child(ren) involved. A scripture I love to lean on in these challenging times is "God is in the midst of her; she shall not be moved. God shall help her"- Psalms 46:5. If you too, overthink like I do, especially in this area, take comfort in knowing that it is okay we drop the ball in trying to be who and what our children want us to be. Being a mom is a twenty-four hour, seven days a week gig and God desires us to just be who He created us to be, and that is His. So, mama's love God, your family, and love yourself! It is hard to give pieces of yourself away to smaller versions of us if you do not love yourself first.

● ● ● ● ● ● ● ● ● ● ● ● ● ● ● ● ● ● ● ● ● ● ● ● ● ● ● ● ● ●

Facebook: Thewaitingroom

Email: Thewaitingroom4923@gmail.com

Thewaitingroom4923.space

# Give yourself a
## *Moment!*

*How did this relate to you? Jot it down below.*

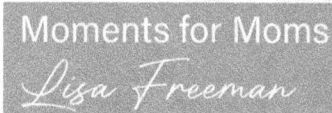

# *Day Seven*

There are so many thoughts and memories that come across my mind as I begin to share with you "my moments" as a mom. First, I truly believe God handpicked us to become the vessels for our children to be born! Some of us may have adopted children or have had to take on the role of a mom for whatever reason. Either way, our roles should never be taken lightly. The stories shared in this devotional are enough proof of that.

I am Lisa Freeman, wife to the most dedicated and loving husband Jerry (aka Len) Freeman. We've been married for 28 years and have three adult children, Keron 32, J'quan 29, and Jerlisa 27. We also have two grands Jaxtin and Journi, who affectionately call us GG and PopPop. I am a serial entrepreneur of several businesses and I have learned to fully embrace my purpose in life to "Live every day like it's a gift from God." One thing I have learned to rely on and that is, "...**With God all things are possible." (Matthew 19:26 KJV)** Life in the natural does not come with a manual but God's way does. As I practice using the word of God as my guide the more confident I became with my life, my responsibilities, and my purpose.

I became a mom at age seventeen. I had decided to have a child with my then-boyfriend because he wanted to have a child. It all seemed right at the time because I thought I was in love. When really I was hiding behind an abusive and toxic relationship. It wasn't until I gave birth that I realized that I needed to break away and become a responsible parent to my son. I remember thinking I may have sacrificed myself, but I was not willing to sacrifice a toxic environment around my child. I had decided it was my responsibility to move on even if I had to do it alone.

The following year I enrolled in Community College and that's where I met my husband. This time I fell completely in love, and I knew it was a forever love. Two years later we had our second son J'quan and married a year later. We found out a few weeks after our honeymoon we were pregnant again with my daughter Jerlisa. I truly believe that even though I made the decision to become a mother so early in my life, God still had a very specific plan for me. As young women, we look to be loved and sometimes become blinded by the warning signs. However, that doesn't make us unqualified to become the women we are destined to be. I remember reading a portion of scripture from **Psalm 127:3 NIV, Children are a gift from the Lord; they are a reward from him.** It helped me get my joy back that God saw fit for a young mother like me to be rewarded with a gift. This became the turning point for me as I found myself struggling with a medical condition Keron had developed.

We found out that Keron was born with a brain tumor. There were no visible signs of developmental delays or anything until after he turned three. He suddenly began to act strange with his daily routines and activities. I noticed his appetite decreasing and he started to withdraw from playing with his favorite toys. I thought he was just being picky until one day he told me, his head was hurting. I called my mom because you know that's what we do. We tried to think through what it could possibly be. A few days before he had fallen from the swings while we were on the playground. At the time he didn't seem hurt, with no bruises or anything and it wasn't a hard fall. We all agreed to get him examined by a doctor.

I arrived at the hospital and shared my concerns about his behavior and the fall. They responded expeditiously and recommended doing a CT scan and the events after changed my world forever! The Doctors would come in and out of his room talking among themselves, looking at his chart and flipping the paperwork back and forth. Watching them do all that was driving me crazy! I remember having this overwhelming feeling of concern and naturally began to panic. After inquiring to one of the nurses "what was going on?" ... They shared they needed to transfer him to another local hospital for more specialized testing. A few hours later is when we were told about the brain tumor. The doctors assured me it wasn't from the fall because of the size of the tumor. They said it was the size of a grapefruit and it had to be growing probably since birth. I was a babe in Christ, my faith was nowhere where is it today. All of my energy and concerns were about what was happening to my child. I didn't know how to exercise my faith then because I was simply terrified, BUT GOD! I had prayerful parents, aunts/uncles, church family, and friends. I believe this was the beginning of me realizing how merciful God is. I knew it wasn't because of my faith, because I was too scared, but I watched my family and church intercede.

Sometimes tragedy and failure are our best teachers in life. The things we fear the most end up teaching us how to walk by faith. It definitely changed my life and pushed me closer to God. My son underwent two major brain surgeries plus chemo treatments. The risks that were involved were very serious for a three-year-old. They warned me that he may not be able to speak or even remember me afterward. All I wanted them to do was fix it. Prayer changes everything because my son came out of major surgery, looked me eye to eye, and said, "Momma where have you been?" Glory to

God I was filled with so much gratefulness! I knew God had released His blessing over his life! It changed my faith and I wanted to change my life to glorify God!

Let me also share this, let's not forget I had two other babies to care for as well. I had J'quan and Jerlisa who were also toddlers at the time. Having to maintain caring for them at home and practically living in and out of the hospital for weeks at a time was very emotional. Thank God for "mothers" because mine was there through it all! If it wasn't for my mother, Ann Williams I know it would have been extremely hard to manage what I needed to do for my family and multiple responsibilities I had at the time. Yet we continued to experience God's faithfulness through it all.

As I matured in the Word I also became more focused on personal development. One day while talking to a friend about family life and challenges with our children. I remember saying to her; "God should have given us a parenting manual to deal with these kids!" We laughed as we encouraged one another. Then she shared with me a book written by Florence Littauer called, "Personality Plus," which she read that helped her at the time. She shares her study of character traits and understanding your child's individuality. I was very interested so I purchased the book that day. Let's just say my marriage changed and how I interacted with my children changed; all for good! I was pleasantly impressed that after learning their personality traits I experienced more sanity to say the least. It was like I had superpowers, and no one knew about it but me! I had gained so much revelation from my past experiences with walking by faith and then the revelation about learning about their individual personalities. It gave me the tools I needed at that time to understand that all behavior wasn't disobedience. For some children, you have to set boundaries, and for some, you need to give them options.

So many things started to add up with how we were parenting them, and this ended up being sort of like that manual I had jokingly shared with my friend! I even discovered my personality and my husband's personality. It went deeper than that, as I began my entrepreneurial journey and working with multiple people. Some of that same information assisted me with understanding different personalities and how to effectively work with different people.

Overall the most valuable lesson I have learned as a Mom is to put my trust in God and that the word of God was the ultimate manual I needed to live by. Then to understand that it was okay to relinquish my super-mom badge. I realized I'm not supposed to "fix" everything, it was my job to train them up in the way they should go. We tend to have certain visions for our children and God may have a different path for them. This scripture has helped encourage me a lot, **ALL things work together for our good to them that love God, to them who are called according to his purpose. (Romans 8:28 KJV)** It may not look like it's working through our eyes at the time, but God is! We need to embrace the fact that what may have worked for one child may not work for the other ones. Also, be open to learning different things from other resources to assist you along the way. The help you are looking for may come in a way you least expect. Don't get stuck always trying to deliver being the strongest all the time. Being their protector, teacher, advocator, role model, sports mom, chef, advisor, giver, and all the other roles required of us, we then get caught up in mundane routines and forget we are entitled to happiness too.

Take time for you to receive it as well. Spend time doing things that bring you peace, make you laugh, and bring you joy, whatever that is, do more of that! For me it's waking up every day practicing being grateful, praying and studying the word of God, and affirming my thoughts as I move throughout the day. I also treat myself to massages, relaxing in a hot lavender bath with a good book, DYI projects, working out, and shopping time! Doing the things that help me relax and take breaks. I have come to the conclusion the more time I spend balancing self-care; I experience being more at peace with life even when the challenges come.

We don't realize how preordained our lives already are until we learn to rely on scriptures like **Jeremiah 29:11 (NIV), For I know the plans I have for you, declares the Lord, plans to prosper you and not to harm you, plans to give you hope and a future.** We may not always understand the reason we have to deal with so much all the time, but God knows, and His plans are full of hope for prosperity! Our purpose in life is in the heart of God. Learning to lean into your purpose and being true to yourself daily helps to maximize your peace and confidence. It has helped me to learn to let some things go and give them to God in prayer so I can live, embrace and enjoy being my true authentic self!

I will leave you with one of my quotes, move forward in faith, smile and laugh a lot, and treat yourself as often as you want because **"There is no one like YOU and that's your superpower"**

www.looksbylisafreeman.com

Facebook:

-@Lisa Freeman

-@Looks by Lisa Freeman

Instagram:

-@thisis_lisafreeman

-@shoplisafreeman

-@marriage_that_works

# Give yourself a *Moment!*

*How did this relate to you? Jot it down below.*

Moments for Moms
*Cheryl Bowman*

# Day Eight

Hi moms! I'm a single mom of 2 sons, ages 23 and 20. I was an educator for 16 years before switching careers. Throughout the years I have had the pleasure of assisting with the raising of other children as well.

The biggest struggle I have had recently as a mother is knowing when to let your "baby" be an adult. Recently my 20-year-old got married. That was a joyous occasion as well as a heartbreaking one. My baby was officially not my baby anymore. I had to allow his wife to now be the one to take care of him. She is the one who will help him make decisions, take care of him when he is sick, cook for him, and one day have my grandchildren. That was and sometimes still is the hardest thing for me to do. I mean, how do I let go?

Despite everything, I had to give my son a chance to be the man I raised him to be. They moved into their own place recently and to help get pass the sad feeling of 'abandonment' I decided it was time for mama to get a "life." I put my life on hold when I gave birth to my youngest son. I wanted to focus on raising my then two men-in-training. I have now enrolled in school again and I have started going out more to hang with friends. I also started a new job which brought on new adventures. Do something that you have put off for a while due to your full job as a mom. Read a good book, do a jigsaw puzzle or join a gym. Either way, focus on yourself for a change.

My advice to you is to allow your children to take off the training wheels and show you the adult you raised them to be. As a mom, we don't want our children to fail but they can't succeed in life without a few bumps and bruises. The only thing we can do is be there to help bandage them up if they need it.

*"Life doesn't come with a manual, it comes with a mother."-*

**UNKNOWN**

• • • • • • • • • • • • • • • • • • • • • • • • • • • • • • • • • • • •

EMAIL: cherylbowman98@gmail.com

*How did this relate to you? Jot it down below.*

Moments for Moms
Shanice Spence

# Day Nine

Hello, my name is Shanice Spence. I am a wife to Daniel for 10 years, a mother to Shatina who is 21, and Kirshaun who is 15. I am also a granddaughter, daughter, sister, aunt, niece, nurse, and pastor. In my spare time, I love to shop, do arts and crafts, travel, and spend time with my family. I love helping others and watching them overcome struggles when they often feel alone and watching others discover why they were created.

As a mother, I have struggled with many things. The one struggle that would stick out for me the most, is trying to be that "perfect" mother all while trying to make sure my children do not follow in my footsteps. What is perfect? There is no such thing as "perfect." As a mother, you always want your child/children to go further and accomplish much more than you have ever accomplished. I had both of my children out of wedlock, and both have two different fathers. I had my first child at 17 and my second one at 23. I had to learn how to grow up FAST!!! I was trying to balance "motherhood" all while learning when to say "no" and when to say "yes." Most of the time my answer would be "no" because I feared my children becoming a statistic in this cruel world. I did not want to fail as a parent.

I had to learn how to overcome the struggles that I had within myself. I had to realize that I could no longer allow fear to grip me. If I say that I am a child of God, then I need to believe what I speak. According to Proverbs 22:6 in the King James Bible, it states "Train up a child in the way he should go and when he is old, he will not depart from it." This verse of text is not gender-specific. I had to learn to put my total trust in God. There are days when I am tested by this, and I often find myself reciting scripture.

I also had to learn how to overcome the lies that I had often battled with and constantly fed myself. The lies that would say, my children would not amount to anything, or no one had loved my children. It wasn't until I learned to love myself completely is when everything changed. You overcome lies by feeding them the truth and positivity.

If I could give any advice to moms, I mentioned earlier that no one is perfect, but in the eyes of God, we are perfect. According to Psalm 139:14, we are fearfully and wonderfully made. Everything that God created is by His perfect design. I encourage you to reach out to others that have walked in your shoes and have experienced what you may be going through or have gone through. It is very much okay to seek professional help if needed but just remember in seeking help, seasons in life often do change. There will be good days and bad days but with those bad days, character is built. Make sure lines of communication are always open. Lastly, trust your children unless they prove otherwise, your mistakes do not determine who they are, what they would do, or who they will become.

• • • • • • • • • • • • • • • • • • • • • • • • • • • • • •

Email: s.e.davis@spartans.nsu.edu

Moments for Moms - *Shanice Spence* | 61

Give yourself a
*Moment!*

*How did this relate to you? Jot it down below.*

Moments for Moms
*Tonisha Morton*

# Day Ten

I remember when my children were younger and they didn't realize I had a name, so they called me 'Mommy Morton.' However, my first name is Tonisha! I become a mom the day before my 19th birthday. I am now 34 years young with 3 wonderful and very adventurous children (1 girl and 2 boys). My absolute favorite hobby to do with my children is traveling and creating memories. I'm the epitome and the voice of single moms. Yes, I do toot my own horn and I am very cocky when it comes to motherhood.

**Single mother chaos**

Raising children alone isn't the Ideal situation. But I've learned to live with it, I've learned to cope with it, and I've learned to grow from it. Raising my children became very programmed and routine over time. My behavior became repetitive to the needs of my children. Certainly, there's no way to express or put into words the struggles of single motherhood. The chaos can intensify in a massive way over time. I faced so many questions and judgmental eyes looking me up and down while holding my children. I wasn't allowed to be sick, and I wasn't allowed to take a break. Everyone would look me in my face and say, "This is what you signed up for, so deal with it."

I overcame this difficult challenge and the judgmental looks once I introduced Mommy Morton to Tonisha Morton. I chose to collide the woman I was before children into the new me, the mommy me. When Mommy Morton met Tonisha Morton things began to make sense. Although there was a long road ahead of me, I felt confident.

This was the confidence I witnessed in myself. Every day for a year straight I would play Tupac's 'Keep Your Head.' Listening to this song gave me so much hope and enthusiasm. I learned that you have to find your own motivation, your own 'Why,' your own strength and happiness. Listening to this song reassured me that not all men are the same and some do care about single motherhood. People say music is therapy, and it's true. I encourage every mother to provide herself with inspiration through music. It's important to be mindful of what you listen to. Find uplifting, positive, and encouraging music, not music that reminds you of your current situation. Don't subject yourself to one genre of music. Certainly listening to music will take you to another place. You have to ask yourself what place you want to be in. Do you want a constant reminder of where you are or would you like a reminder of where you're going?

Each and every mom, single or not, you deserve a daily break. Even if it's 20 minutes to listen to your motivational playlist. Go to your safe place in your home or office and sing and dance. Remember this quote by Mark Twain, "Dance like nobody is watching, love like you've never been hurt, sing like nobody's listening, live like is heaven on earth." Shower yourself with love every day. Brace yourself, feel the music and meditate on it.

Peace and Love

Sincerely Tonisha

Facebook: Tonisha Morton

IG: Sincerelytonisha

Email: tonishamorton@gmail.com

# Give yourself a
## *Moment!*

*How did this relate to you? Jot it down below.*

Moments for Moms
*Jaccarri Woodson*

# *Day Eleven*

My name is Jaccarri Woodson, and I am 35 years old. Born and raised in Williamsburg, VA to the late Darryl and Melissa Woodson. I grew up with children all around me because my parents would take in young mothers and their children so that the mothers could finish school and not be worried that their child(ren) was taken care of. As a young girl, I was always the babysitter so when I got older and married children were the last thing on my mind. However, after two years of being married, I found myself pregnant and awaiting a beautiful baby girl.

Out of all the things I wanted to do with my child I struggled with feeling worthy to be her mother internally. I was not blessed with the "skin to skin" connection they said that you would get when you first hold the baby. After 18 hours of labor with this child, I was not mentally prepared for what was to come. I wanted to be a good mother and I think I am, but initially, it was a struggle to think I could handle what it took being a mother. Internally I cried because I felt like this was happening blindly even though I knew what to do. I often said to myself, "Will she be happy to call me mom?"

Over and over, I would rehearse to myself "You were made for this!" Every morning as I pumped one breast, and she was being fed off the other I would stare into her eyes and pray that I make her proud to be Jaccarri Woodson's daughter. The constant reminder that God will not put more on me than I can bear (1 Corinthians

10:13) kept me going to overcome this struggle of not feeling worthy. To continue to reach heights, jump hurdles, and dodge bullets that continue to happen in life, your child sees and hears you and is proud to call you mother.

I encourage you to keep pushing and know that there is nothing that you cannot do. Being a mother may not always feel like the best job but keep pushing. Being a mother may not be the easiest task but keep pushing because you were graced for this. There is nothing or no one that will take away what God has graced you for! **Keep Pushing!**

• • • • • • • • • • • • • • • • • • • • • • • • • • • • • •

**Facebook:** Jaccarri Woodson

**Instagram:** @jaccarriwoodson

**YouTube:** @jaccarriwoodson

*How did this relate to you? Jot it down below.*

Moments for Moms
*Cyteese Alexander*

# Day Twelve

Hello Moms, let me first start by introducing myself, my name is Cyteese Alexander. I always start off by saying I am a daughter of the King. I am a wife, and mother of 4, and did I mention a 2x author? I am a born leader who is on a mission to inspire others by sharing my story of survival, restoration, deliverance, and healing. Having a heart of gold is just one of the things that I love about myself. I am setting out to challenge others to stop viewing themselves as inferior and focusing on the opinions of others. My goal is to help others see themselves the way God sees them.

I do not like to use the word struggle, so I will say challenges. So, one of the challenges I have faced while being a mom is finding the balance of having time for myself. Yes, the word self-care is so hard for me. I am always in mommy mode where I find it hard to find that time for "MYSELF." I am that mom that will make sure that my kids are ok, and I will take my last to be sure they are taken care of. I know I have witnesses that can relate to this challenge. But no matter how strong we are, or portray ourselves to be, I am learning that it is important to pause, take a step back, look in the mirror, and say to myself, "It is ok to take care of YOU."

The steps that I am taking to overcome that challenge is learning to take the time out for MYSELF. I wake up every day and I am learning and being consistent in saying affirmations. Saying things like "I am enough," or " I deserve all that God has for me," and so many more have helped me tremendously. The times I get my nails and feet done, or buy myself a new outfit, that is self-care for me. I do all the things I can every day to get my mind together. Your mind is one of the things the enemy attempts to play with. He tries to talk you out of what you deserve and what God says you can have.

First, what I will tell moms from my personal experiences is to remind yourself, that "YOU," deserve all of the good things that come into your life. Secondly, it's important to know that those times you are running on empty, to know your boundaries. A car cannot run on empty for too long, eventually, it will come to a stop. That is the way our bodies run, if you are not being filled by a good book, an inspirational word, or having a "YOU" day, no matter what it may be, then you won't be able to be a mom at your best potential. No matter how hard you try. Take it from me, you must make sure your mind, body, and spirit are in place so that you can be the best mom and come up with the best version of yourself.

**The 3 best pieces of advice that I could provide from my personal experience is:**

1) You must know that you deserve every good and perfect gift from God. You alone are "ENOUGH!"

2) Even though we wear many hats, we have to first know that before we can be effective in our roles for everyone else, we have to remember that we are women, and taking care of ourselves is important.

3) The final piece of advice that I can provide to all these amazing women out there who may be reading this is to know that you alone beautiful, are "enough!"

Facebook: Cyteese Alexander

IG: Iam_cyteese

www.iamcyteese.com

# Give yourself a
## *Moment!*

*How did this relate to you? Jot it down below.*

Moments for Moms
*Ronjeanna Harris*

# Day Thirteen

Hello moms, my name is Ronjeanna Harris, I'm a kingdom believer, servant, ordained evangelist, wife, mother, and business owner. I love serving and helping others with positive solutions. My business is Just Jeanna's Skin Care LLC providing all-natural skincare products and services. I'm the founder and executive director of Jeanna's iFeed nonprofit where we provide cook meals in the community along with other services. I have over 22 years in the health field. I am a Skilled LPN by trade.

One of the struggles I faced was becoming a mother too young. I had my first child at 16 years old. At that age, I was still maturing in thought and mentality. This created so many insecurities for me that I didn't realize it back then. I had low self-esteem and often wanted to be unnoticed because of that. I had postpartum depression that didn't get recognized by those closest to me. I was so young that many thought I was just acting like a typical teenager. I was a young single parent until I met my husband in 2001.

**Journey to becoming an effective overcomer as a mother!**

I finally realized that my healing was necessary to rear my children as the Bible instructs us. The first step to healing is to acknowledge that something is consuming you from operating in a healthy well-being. I started slowly verbalizing my true feelings so proper help could be offered to aide me in my healing journey. I started paying attention to patterns that promoted dysfunction during my struggle. I thought about the impact of not properly overcoming could have on my children and generations down the line. This created a deeper passion to overcome any obstacle I was facing as a mother. I thought about the impact not properly overcoming obstacles in my life could have on my children and future generations.

Becoming selfless in operation to master this challenge was the direction that was most rewarding to accomplish this. I was determined to be in a healthy state to be the best mother I could be. I got under local mentoring programs in my area for mothers. I remember that God is a keeper and even in my darkest moments I kept that in my thought process. I embraced healthy support. I did not allow my circumstances to keep me stuck and depressed.

**Effective Nuggets to the reader!**

- ❖ Always believe in yourself and the uniqueness that God has created in you as a mother.
- ❖ Never embrace overwhelming situations that may occur during the day without a clear thought process.
- ❖ Put God first in every decision you make in parenthood.

• • • • • • • • • • • • • • • • • • • • • • • • • • • • • • • • •

www.justjeannas.com

Email: justjeannasskincare@gmail.com

Email: jeannasifeed@gmail.com

Facebook/Instagram: Just Jeanna's Skin Care

Facebook/Instagram: Jeanna's iFeed

Give yourself a
*Moment!*

*How did this relate to you? Jot it down below.*

Moments for Moms
*Juanita N. Woodson*

# Day Fourteen

Mom, wife, auntie, sister, god mommy, friend; more importantly, Juanita. I am a woman who wears a lot of hats proudly. I own Grace 4 Purpose, Publishing Co where we help aspiring authors and writers publish their books with purpose. After writing and publishing my own books I knew I was created to help other women do the same. The work that I do on a daily basis as a coach, motivator, accountability coach, and publisher has connected me with so many different moms and it gives me great joy to help them share their stories to help someone else.

There are many different hats that I wear on a daily basis, and I believe that being a mother is one that has really helped me to walk in my purpose. As my son has gotten older our life has gone through different transitions. Along with the transitions we have faced together, there are also social pressures of the world; some I never had to face growing up that my son faces on a daily basis. With all of these changes and pressures, it can become hard to deal with the up-and-down mood swings that come out of nowhere, the lack of communication, and also the emotions of seeing my son grow into his own independent person.

I remember my son always wanting to be by my side; like I couldn't get him out of my bed. He isn't as connected at my hip as he once was. As he has gotten older and with some of the things that he has faced in his life, there are times when I just don't understand.

Sometimes I don't know the right words to say to comfort him, or I pry because he isn't saying too much, and I just want to know what is going on in his head. As a mother, I am constantly just praying for the safety and protection of my teenage son, not just from the external things in the world, but also for his mind.

I started to find different ways to connect with my son, as your child gets older and as their independence grows the things they like to do will change; so it was important for me to understand that I had to get to know my son every single day. Our children are human so as we grow and change, so do they. Having this understanding helped me to practice patience and grace more than ever. I have also been reminded of why it is so important to allow God to lead the way in parenting daily. It's important to understand that none of us have all the answers when it comes to being a mom, so who is better to help us than the one that created us?

As I have grown as a mother there is so much advice that I could share, but I will leave you with the three most important pieces right now. First, prayer is so important for our babies; I almost feel like it is a lost thing. I know for a fact that I still have my mama and grandmother's prayers covering me to this day. Mamas, start your day with prayer over your babies, yourself, and your entire household. Secondly, lead by example, your child will learn so many lessons in life by how you handle things in your own life. Lastly, fail forward. We don't know everything, each day that your child grows you grow too. Take the time necessary to be patient with yourself and extend that same patience and grace to them.

• • • • • • • • • • • • • • • • • • • • • • • • • • • • • •

I would love to connect with you, mama! Follow me on social media!

IG- @_juanitanicole_

IG- @grace4purposeco

Facebook: @grace4purposeco

Facebook: Author Juanita N. Woodson

Email: contact@grace4purposeco.com

www.grace4purposeco.com

# Give yourself a
## *Moment!*

*How did this relate to you? Jot it down below.*

Moments for Moms

# DAY FIFTEEN

*Mama, surround yourself with a tribe that will encourage you, pray for you and push you to walk in your God-ordained purpose.* As a mother, it is imperative that we walk in our purpose so that our children can see what life looks like when we follow the plan God has for us. Jeremiah 29:11 reminds us that God has plans for us, not just any plans for us, but plans that will prosper us. And the good thing about following God's plan as we walk in our purpose is that His plan won't harm us. As a mother, it is so important to remember that. *Raising children in this world full of unknowns can be scary, but when you have your foundation built with faith in God, it gives you room to breathe and give yourself a minute!*

*As you take time to give yourself a minute today and each day, speak positive affirmations over your life, pray and stay in your Word. We have left you with some to carry with you each day.*

"Healing is just one of the many ways God has graced us to show His love." – **Catrina Jackson**

"Always believe in yourself and the uniqueness that God has created in you as a mother." - **Ronjenna Harris**

"Our purpose in life is in the heart of God. Learning to lean into your purpose and being true to yourself daily helps to maximize your peace and confidence." -**Lisa Freeman**

"Allow your children to take off the training wheels and show you the adult you raised them to be." -**Cheryl Bowman**

"Trust your children unless they prove otherwise, your mistakes do not determine who they are, what they would do, or who they will become." -**Shanice Spence**

"You have to ask yourself what place you want to be in. Do you want a constant reminder of where you are or would you like a reminder of where you're going?" -**Tonisha Morton**

"Be at peace knowing that the prayers you prayed while your child was in the womb will manifest and God will keep His promise." -**Nikki Lawrence**

"It is okay to not know all the right answers. It is okay to make mistakes, no one is perfect. It is okay to fall but it is not okay to stay down." -**AuJahna'e Coady**

"Love God, your family, and love yourself. It is hard to give pieces of yourself away to smaller versions of us if you do not love yourself first." -**Shatera Martz**

"Help does not mean you are weak or unable, it just means that you

are strong enough to place yourself in someone else's hands to be cared for. No matter what you do, just let someone be there for you."
**-Marquese Hannah**

"Even on the challenging days, I am learning it is essential to watch what you say because each word out of your mouth has an assignment." **-Ebony S. Bailey**

"There is nothing or no one that will take away what God has graced you for! Keep Pushing!" **-Jaccarri Woodson**

"It's important to know your boundaries during those times you are running on empty. A car cannot run on empty for too long, eventually, it will come to a stop." **-Cyteese Alexander**

"Lead by example, your child will learn so many lessons in life by how you handle things in your own life." **-Juanita Woodson**

# Give yourself a
## *Moment!*

*How did this relate to you? Jot it down below.*

# Father,

Thank You for giving us the gift of life, we don't take it for granted. As we continue to grow as mothers, direct our path daily. Provide us with the insight that we need to raise the next generation so that they will follow after You. Father, we know that You make all things work together for our good, so we pray for the mama that needs that reminder, we pray that You remind her that You are with her every step of the way. We pray that You open up the doors and the resources for each mama that reads this book to care for her family and the guidance to walk in her purpose. Fill her with Your joy, Your peace, and Your purpose. Thank you for giving us a moment to seek You each and every day!

*-In Jesus Name, Amen!*

Grace4Purposeco.com

www.ingramcontent.com/pod-product-compliance
Lightning Source LLC
Chambersburg PA
CBHW051947160426
43198CB00013B/2340